NEW VANGUARD • 142

TUDOR WARSHIPS (1)

Henry VIII's Navy

ANGUS KONSTAM   ILLUSTRATED BY TONY BRYAN

First published in Great Britain in 2008 by Osprey Publishing,
PO Box 883, Oxford, OX1 9PL, UK
PO Box 3985, New York, NY 10185-3985, USA
Email: info@ospreypublishing.com

Osprey Publishing is part of the Osprey Group.

Transferred to digital print on demand 2014.

First published 2008
2nd impression 2014

Printed and bound in Great Britain

A CIP catalogue record for this book is available from
the British Library.

ISBN: 978 1 84603 251 6

Page layout by Melissa Orrom Swan, Oxford
Index by Alan Thatcher
Typeset in Myriad Pro and Sabon
Originated by PPS Grasmere Ltd.

The Woodland Trust
Osprey Publishing are supporting the Woodland Trust, the UK's
leading woodland conservation charity, by funding the
dedication of trees.

www.ospreypublishing.com

Editor's note
For ease of comparison between types, imperial
measurements are used almost exclusively throughout this
book. The following data will help in converting the imperial
measurements to metric:
1 mile = 1.6km
1lb = 0.45kg
1 yard = 0.9m
1ft = 0.3m
1in. = 2.54cm/25.4mm
1 gal = 4.5 liters
1 ton (US) = 0.9 tonnes

Glossary

Bowsprit	a large spar projecting out over the bow (or stem) of the vessel.
Forecastle	Pronounced fo'c'scle, this refers to the castle-like structure built over the bows of the ship, used to house soldiers or weaponry during a battle. The name reflects their perceived value as defensive redoubts if a ship was attacked.
Keelson	An internal keel (or stringer), bolted to the top of the keel to provide additional strength and support to the hull.
Lateen-rigged	A lateen sail was a narrow, triangular sail, first developed in the Mediterranean, the forward end of which pointed to the ship's deck, and the other end terminated in a high peak. A lateen-rigged mast was one fitted exclusively with a lateen sail.
Mainmast	The main mast of the ship.
Mizzen	A mast sited behind the mainmast on a sailing ship. In some Tudor ships this was the aftermost mast on the ship, while on some larger vessels another even smaller mast – the Bonadventure mizzen – was set behind it.
Mothballed	A modern naval phrase, reflecting the situation when a ship was stripped of its rigging, guns and stores. In this condition it was kept at anchor and maintained by a skeleton crew. In effect it was being kept in storage, or 'kept in mothballs'. A more contemporary phrase was that the ship was being kept 'in ordinary'.
Sterncastle	The after version of the forecastle, situated behind the waist of the ship.
Topsail	The topmost sail on a mast.
Transom Stern	A name given to the flat stern of the ship, taking its name from the horizontal timbers bolted to the sternpost of the ship to produce this flat stern.
Tumblehome	The inward-sloping curve of a ship's hull, where the sides of the ship are brought inwards towards the centreline of the vessel, from the widest point of the ship's beam – which is usually along the waterline. This made the width of the main deck narrower than that of the lower decks.

CONTENTS

TUDOR WARSHIPS (1) HENRY VIII'S NAVY

INTRODUCTION

Historians like to bandy around the word 'revolution', particularly when it comes to matters military or naval. Any dramatic and wide-ranging change in the status quo has warranted the term, from the 'military revolution' of the later Renaissance to the 'naval revolution' of the mid-19th century. However, few periods warrant the term's use more than the era of the Tudors. Their reign spanned a century that witnessed profound religious, economic, social, cultural, political and military transformations.

As in other technological areas, the art of shipbuilding and the science of gun founding both underwent major changes during this period, and increasingly the introduction of artillery pieces onto ships exerted a powerful influence over naval design. Few monarchs were more aware of the power of naval artillery than King Henry VIII (r.1509–47) of England. While his father, Henry VII (r.1485–1509), had encouraged the introduction of guns into ships, the younger Henry had royal warships designed specifically to accommodate heavy ordnance. This process of marrying artillery and warships and designing ships as gun platforms would reach a peak during the reign of his daughter Elizabeth I (r.1558–1603).

As a historian I have had a long-standing fascination with this crucial period of naval development, and two decades ago it formed the subject of my Master's degree. Since then new research and the science of underwater archaeology have revealed fresh information, and it is hoped these books will provide a useful summary of current thinking, divided into two volumes. This first volume covers the early development of the fleet under the guidance of Henry VII and Henry VIII. The second will then deal with the development of the navy during the reign of Elizabeth I.

Henry VII gradually built up the strength of the Tudor Navy Royal, and commissioned the two prestigious great carracks, *Sovereign* and *Regent*. (Stratford Archive)

SHIP DESIGN

From the time Henry VII (Henry Tudor) inherited the old Yorkist fleet in 1485 until the death of Henry VIII's young son Edward VI in 1553, the nature of

warships changed completely, from the late-medieval vessels designed for carrying mêlée troops into battle, to the purpose-built gun platforms of the fleet designed under the guidance of Henry VIII. For the sake of simplicity we can break this development down into three fairly distinct phases: late-medieval warships, carracks, and the adaptation phase.

Late medieval warships

Before we look at the development of warships during the reigns of the Tudor kings, we need to take a brief look at the changing face of European ship design during the 15th century. Evidence for the development of shipping during this period is provided by illustrations, paintings, carvings, ship models, the written record and even by some archaeological sources. What these tell us is that during the decades preceding Henry VII's accession, the design of the late-medieval warship was changing to reflect new innovations, and to accommodate the increased role of missile fire in combat. In addition, two distinct shipbuilding traditions existed – one in northern Europe, the other in the Mediterranean. During the 15th century the growth of maritime commerce led to the two traditions borrowing ideas from each other, thus creating a new shipbuilding style which drew upon the best elements from each school. By 1485 a fusion of both traditions was well under way – a process that would accelerate during the early 16th century.

The northern shipbuilding tradition had already produced the *cog* – the workhorse of the northern European sea lanes in the 14th century. It was also a type of vessel that lent itself to naval use, and so mercantile cogs were

A detail from *Henry VIII's Embarkation for France*, a painting by an unknown artist depicting events in 1520, when Henry VIII met Francis I at 'The Field of the Cloth of Gold'. The four-masted vessel in the background is probably meant to represent the *Henri Grâce à Dieu*, even though the deep draught of the 1,000-ton warship meant she was unable to enter Dover harbour, where this scene is set. Taken from a reproduction of the original painting in Hampton Court Palace. (Stratford Archive)

commonly pressed into service as warships. The design roots of the cog can be traced back to the *knorrs* used by Scandinavian traders from the 8th century. Both vessels shared the same basic form of construction, square sails, and even possessed ancestry in the *nef*, a vessel type that served as a link between the earlier and later designs. A typical cog was a squat-looking vessel with a broad beam, a rounded bow and stern, and often pronounced forecastle and sterncastle structures. She usually carried a single mast amidships, although some 14th- and 15th-century illustrations depict vessels with a small mizzen mast.

Cogs were 'clinker-built', meaning that the lower edge of each plank in the hull's side overlapped the plank below it. In North America the technique is called 'lapstrake' construction. The join between the two planks was caulked, then fastened together using a clinker (or clinch nail), a term derived from the Middle English word *clinken*, meaning clinched. Vessels were built from the keel up, the planks fastened to a series of internal frames that provided rigidity to the structure. These frames ended in pronounced stem and stern posts, rising from the keel by means of intermediate sections known as hooks. In 14th-century Germanic cogs, these stem and stern posts were relatively straight, the latter incorporating a rudder that ran up the stern from keel to gunwale. Fifteenth-century cogs appear to have had smaller rudders, and the vessels themselves appear to have been more rounded than those of a century before. In particular, pictorial evidence suggests that by the middle of the 15th century bows possessed a very pronounced, rounded curve.

However, by that stage the cog had given way to a new vessel type, an enlarged version of the cog sometimes known as the *hulk* (a vessel type called the *nao* in Spain and Portugal). It came about as a result of the interplay between the northern and southern European shipbuilding traditions. Mediterranean vessels used a 'carvel construction' technique, where the hull

THE *HENRI GRACE A DIEU*, 1525

One of the most ambitious warships built during the Tudor period, her construction was probably a direct response to the building of the *Great Michael* (1512) by King James IV of Scotland. Unfortunately, it was three decades before she was called upon to fire her guns in anger, and she spent most of her career mothballed. She was designed more for prestige than for any naval value she might have, and in 1520 she escorted Henry VIII from Dover to Calais for his meeting with Francis I at 'The Field of the Cloth of Gold'. Even then her draught prohibited her from entering either harbour. While her appearance was impressive, the cost of operating her in peacetime was considered prohibitive, and she came to be seen as something of a white elephant. The inset shows one of the wrought-iron breech-loading 'great pieces' she carried, mounted on a carriage based on one recovered from the wreck of the *Mary Rose* (1545).

SPECIFICATIONS – *HENRI GRACE A DIEU*

Type: A 'great ship' (carrack) nicknamed the '*Great Harry*'. Built 1514 (Woolwich).

Displacement: 1,000 tons.*

Keel length: 130ft approx.

Beam: 50ft approx.

Armament: 80 guns (51 heavy, the rest swivel guns; her total listed armament of 112 guns included the handguns carried on board).

Crew (1536): 700 men (including 400 soldiers and 40 gunners).

Service notes: Rebuilt 1539. Participated in the battle off Portsmouth, 1545. Renamed *Edward* (1547), destroyed by accidental fire, 1553.

* Some early sources (based on a different displacement system) give this as 1,500 tons.

A pair of Tudor warships – a detail taken from an English pilot's guide, c.1525. Both small vessels are pierced with gunports on the level of the main gundeck and have piercings on the forecastle and sterncastle structures that may be firing ports for swivel guns. (Pierpont Morgan Library)

planks abutted rather than overlapped each other. By the 14th century the two schools began borrowing techniques from one other, as demonstrated by the introduction of carvel construction into France and the Iberian Peninsula, and the use of the sternpost rudder (as found on the cog) in Mediterranean ships. The hulk combined the best elements of both traditions, permitting the construction of ships with larger hulls than previous clinker-built vessels, and using a combination of northern and southern European sailing rigs and steering systems to make the ship handle more efficiently than earlier vessels. In 16th-century England the term 'hulk' was used to describe a northern European but non-English merchantman, while by the end of the century the term was reserved for worn-out (and usually large) vessels – a term which remains in use today.

Although there is some debate whether all hulks were carvel-built, other elements of Mediterranean design were embraced wholeheartedly. The hull was essentially a larger version of the earlier ship type, although more rounded. Like the cog, the hulk employed a square mainsail, but it also carried a second Mediterranean-style lateen-rigged sail on an after mast – the mizzen. Other square sails could be carried on a foremast and above the lateen sail on the mizzen mast, while some hulks also carried topsails, and a spritsail suspended from a bowsprit. The crucial element about this new design was that while the standard cog only carried one mast, these new vessels were fitted with two or even three masts. These extra masts and sails meant the ship was faster, capable of sailing closer to the wind than purely square-rigged ships, and above all it now had the ability to sail farther afield – into the Baltic, the Mediterranean or to parts unknown. The ability to sail closer to the direction of the oncoming wind obviously made it easier to sail to destinations that had hitherto been difficult to reach because of the prevailing winds. This seemingly minor advance would transform the maritime world.

The carrack

We don't know exactly when the *carrack* first made its appearance, but as early as 1304 the Florentine chronicler Giovanni Villani claimed that Italian shipwrights were copying the design of the Basque cog, producing a ship type referred to as a *cocha*. Only a few tantalizing pictorial references of the early cochas survive, but by 1340 the largest of these were known as the cocha *baronesche*, which were bigger, deeper-hulled versions of the original Basque cog. These were almost certainly designed with two masts, carrying a combination of a square-rigged mainsail and a lateen sail on the mizzen. By the later 14th century the term 'carrack' was being used by the English to describe Genoese trading ships of this type, although there is no evidence of them sailing as far north as the British Isles until after the turn of the century. In the Iberian peninsula the same vessel was known as the *nao*, although the term was also applied to the Spanish versions of the northern European hulk. In effect, during the 15th century the early carrack, the *nao* and the hulk all referred to similar general ship types.

While there is evidence of two-masted cochas sailing within the Mediterranean during the later 14th century, their first detailed mention in English records came in 1410, when a two-masted Genoese carrack was captured by English pirates, and ownership was later claimed by the English Crown. Another similar carrack was mentioned in official records the following year. By 1417 Henry V (r.1413–22) had acquired eight Genoese carracks that had been hired by the French, and these were added to his nascent royal fleet. Six of them were described as vessels displacing around 500 tons, and fitted with two masts – a mainmast and a 'mesan' (mizzen). During the final years of Henry's reign English-built additions to his fleet also sported two masts, suggesting that the cocha design was copied by English royal shipwrights. However, by the end of Henry's reign these same shipwrights had gone one stage further.

A small warship in Dover harbour, a detail from a sketch of *c.*1530. The vessel is pierced with gunports, while soldiers armed with a variety of weapons are shown in the fighting platforms of the forecastle and sterncastle. (British Library)

A year after his victory over the French at the battle of Agincourt (1415), Henry V ordered the construction of two new warships, one of which was built at Bayonne on the coast of Aquitaine, and the other at Southampton in Hampshire. The Southampton ship was the larger of the two, and when she was launched in 1418 it was recorded that she displaced a record 1,400 tons. Little is known about this monster ship, known as the *Grace Dieu*, save a few surviving inventories made of her stores after she was mothballed in 1420, but fortunately her remains were discovered near Bursledon on the River Hamble, and these were surveyed and sampled at various times from the mid 19th century onwards. They reveal that her hull was clinker-built, with a keel length of around 125ft, and a beam of 50ft. These dimensions make her bigger than any other ship built in the British Isles until the 17th century. A Florentine galley captain provided an eyewitness account of the *Grace Dieu*, adding that she was about 184ft long at deck level, with a mainmast 200ft high and 22ft in circumference.

By comparing the written records with her remains, it becomes clear that the *Grace Dieu* was an early carrack fitted with two masts – a large main and a smaller mizzen. In addition, a bowsprit extended forward from her high fortress-like forecastle. Based on contemporary illustrations of smaller but similarly constructed early vessels, we can assume that her sterncastle (referred to as a 'summer castle') was lower than her forecastle. Interestingly, the Bayonne ship appears to have been carvel-built, which suggests that at least in south-eastern France, Mediterranean methods of construction had already replaced any existing northern European traditions, while the English shipwrights continued to build ships along more traditional lines. Unfortunately, very few English naval records survive for the half century preceding the reign of the Yorkist monarchs Edward IV (r.1461–83) and Richard III (r.1483–85). We therefore have little hard evidence for the transition of the English royal fleet during these crucial decades.

What is clear is that financial hardships and political instability meant that the expansion of a royal fleet was a relatively low priority during this period. However, under Edward IV the fleet was expanded through the purchase and

An English warship being dashed onto the rocks, in a detail from the *Warwick Roll*, *c.*1480. Note the cloth awning (which would have been painted in the earl of Warwick's colours of yellow and blue), and the large pieces of ordnance carried in the ship's waist. The full title of the *Warwick Roll* is *The Pageant of the Birth, Life and Death of Richard Beauchamp, Earl of Warwick*, a series of sketches illustrating incidents in the life of the English nobleman. However, most historians simply call them the *Warwick Roll*. Although Richard Beachamp died in 1439, the sketches were produced much later, and may well have been drawn at the request of one of his children, possibly Anne, the countess of Warwick, the wife of Edward IV's rival at the battle of Barnet. She died in 1493, and the styles of armour and the ships all point to the illustrations being produced some time during the last decade of Anne's life. Alternatively, it might have been produced for her daughter, who became Queen Anne after her husband, Richard, Duke of Gloucester, became King Richard III. She died in 1485, just five months before her husband was killed on the battlefield of Bosworth. (The British Library)

conversion of merchant vessels. In 1480 it consisted of seven carracks, two ships, a caravel and a bark. Of the carracks, two were listed as having been Spanish built, while another was listed as Portuguese. The contemporary difference between a carrack and a 'ship' is not always clear, but generally the latter referred to vessels with a 'full rig' of foremast, mainmast and mizzen mast. While these were fitted with square-rigged sails, lateen-rigged sails were carried by the 1480s, as well as topsails on all three masts.

A *caravel* was a smaller, carvel-built vessel with two or three masts – the latter carrying a lateen sail. This ship type was used extensively by the Portuguese and later the Spanish as a 'ship of discovery'. Finally, a *bark* was another type of three-masted vessel of an indeterminate size, although later barks were usually regarded as small vessels. All three masts carried

B THE *SOVEREIGN*, 1512

The *Regent* and the *Sovereign* were the first warships to be built for the Tudor navy, the latter being constructed on the River Hamble near Southampton under the supervision of Sir Richard Guildeford, the Master of the Ordnance. She entered service in 1489, but we know little about her until after her refit in 1509, when she was re-armed with an impressive array of 14 heavy guns as well as 54 lighter pieces, mainly swivel guns.

She participated in the battle off Brest in 1513, when she was mentioned as one of those ships who attempted to board the French warship *Marie la Cordelière*. After being condemned in 1521 she was left to rot at her moorings on the southern bank of the River Thames at Woolwich, where her remains were discovered in 1912.

SPECIFICATIONS – *SOVEREIGN*

Type: A 'great ship' (carrack) originally known as the *Trinity Sovereign*. Built 1488.

Displacement: 800 tons.

Keel length: 125ft approx.

Beam: 40ft approx.

Armament: 100 guns (mostly swivel guns and handguns) – 69 guns in 1509.

Crew (1513): 700 men (including 400 soldiers and 40 gunners).

Service notes: Rebuilt 1509. Participated in the battle off Brest, 1512. Declared unseaworthy in 1521, and removed from the navy list.

square-rigged sails, the last one on the mizzen being rigged fore and aft, so it resembled a square version of a lateen sail. The *Caravel of Salcombe* was sold following the death of Edward IV, and remained one of only two vessels of this type to be included in the Navy Royal (this was a 14th-century term, not to be superseded by 'Royal Navy' until 1660). The *Bark of Southampton* was renamed the *Bonadventure* during the last years of the century, when she was reclassified as a carrack. This suggests that it was her sailing rig rather than her design that led to her classification as a bark.

Another notable feature of the 15th-century northern European carrack was the configuration of the stern. Hull planking (or 'strakes') was bent round and upwards at the stern, creating a more rounded end than on later vessels. This was also a feature found on contemporary hulks. From 1488 at the latest this practice had been replaced by a simpler form of construction where the strakes were fastened to the after frame, and a flat transom stern added. This simplification was important when it came to constructing heavier-built vessels, designed to absorb the fire of heavy ordnance.

The adaptation phase

The Navy Royal inherited by the first Tudor monarch, Henry VII, was essentially a force of carracks. All but one of its eight vessels were of this ship type, and the exception – a ship called the *Nickolas of London* – was sold off before the end of the year. Two carracks were also disposed of at the same time. Although we know little of their respective sizes, the financial records suggest that all of the remaining five vessels were large, all former merchantmen with high castles fore and aft. All five carried a mixture of 'port pieces' (wrought-iron, breech-loading guns) and smaller swivel pieces. These latter weapons were also breech-loading and usually made from wrought iron,

Henry VII's Navy Royal, 1485–1509

Vessel	Ship type	Entered service	Additional information	Date service ended
Mary of the Tower	Carrack	1478	Former Spanish merchantman. Originally named *Carcyon*	1496
Trinity	Carrack	1478	Former merchantman	1503
Bark of Southhampton	Carrack	1483	Former merchantman. Renamed *Bonadventure*, c.1486	By 1509
Governor	Carrack	1485	Former merchantman	1488
Carvel of Ewe	Carvel	1487	Former merchantman. 180 tons. Rebuilt following fire in 1512, and renamed *Mary and John*	Sold by 1522
Regent	Great Ship	Built 1488	1,000 tons	Lost in action, 1512
Sovereign	Great Ship	Built 1488	800 tons	Stricken in 1521
Michael	Ship	1488	Scottish prize	1513
Margaret	Ship	1490	Scottish prize	by 1509
Mary Fortune	Galleass	Built 1497	80 tons. Sometimes known as *Rose Henry*. Renamed *Swallow* in 1512	1527
Sweepstake	Galleass	Built 1497	80 tons. Sometimes known as *Katherine Pomegranate*	1527
In addition the following former warships of Richard III's fleet were disposed of within a year of Henry VII's accession:				
Martin Garcia	Carrack	1470	Former Portuguese merchantman. Originally named *Garse*	1485
Fawkon	Carrack	1478	Former merchantman	1485
Nickolas of London	Ship	1485	Former merchantman	1485
Grace Dieu	Carrack	1473	Former merchantman	1486

but were small enough to be mounted on a yoke (or swivel mount) on a ship's rail – a bit like a modern machine-gun mounting. One of these carracks, the *Mary of the Tower*, carried no fewer than 58 guns in 1485, the majority of which were either handguns or swivel pieces. Handguns varied in size from small hand-held pieces to larger firearms (known as hackbuts) which resembled modern bazookas, and were fitted with a rest which could be hooked over the ship's rail to help absorb the recoil. Another vessel, a second *Grace Dieu*, acquired in 1473, was listed as carrying 21 such guns in the same Tudor inventory. Illustrations such as those in the *Warwick Roll* and the Flemish engraving entitled *Kraek* (Flemish for carrack) by 'WA' show that these would have been mounted either in the waist or the castles, where they could fire over the top of the gunwale. This configuration was only possible because the guns themselves were light enough to have no influence on the stability of the ship. Clearly, the introduction of larger pieces would make the vessel top-heavy unless a way was found to mount the guns closer to the waterline. The way to achieve this had already been found. The *Kraek* engraving, thought to date from around 1468, shows a large armed merchant vessel with a loading port cut low down in the hull, below the sterncastle. The *Warwick Roll* also includes a depiction of a carrack flying the standard of Richard Neville, Earl

ABOVE LEFT
The opposition: the French warship *Grande Louise* (or *Louise Amirale*), the flagship of Admiral Graville, from a contemporary drawing of her made *c*.1520. Her heavy ordnance appears to be mounted in a fairly haphazard fashion in the ship's waist. (Stratford Archive)

ABOVE RIGHT
In 1912 the remains of a Tudor warship were uncovered during building work on the site of Woolwich Power Station, on the banks of the River Thames. These timbers are believed to be from Henry VII's great carrack *Sovereign*, built in 1488. (Stratford Archive)

Navy Royal at the accession of Henry VIII, 1509				
Vessel	**Ship type**	**Entered service**	**Additional information**	**Date service ended**
Carvel of Ewe	Carvel	1487	Former merchantman. 180 tons. Rebuilt following fire in 1512, and renamed *Mary and John*	Sold *c*.1522
Regent	Great Ship	Built 1488	1,000 tons	Lost in action, 1512
Sovereign	Great Ship	Built 1488	800 tons	Stricken in 1521
Michael	Ship	1488	Scottish prize	1513
Mary Fortune	Galleass	Built 1497	80 tons. Sometimes known as *Rose Henry*. Renamed *Swallow* in 1512	1527
Sweepstake	Galleass	Built 1497	80 tons. Sometimes known as *Katherine Pomegranate*	1527

of Warwick (1428–71), armed with a broadside of five or six port pieces. These are mounted on the deck of the waist, in what appear to be gaps cut in the gunwale. A French depiction of the early 16th century warship *Grande Louise* also shows the heavy ordnance grouped in the waist of the ship.

The next step was the deliberate piercing of the hull to accommodate pieces of ordnance. This development was first depicted in a drawing of a German carrack of around 1490, which showed the vessel pierced with two circular gunports, immediately below the waist. It is unclear whether Henry VII's new warships *Sovereign* and *Regent*, laid down in 1486–87, were designed specifically to carry large port pieces, but while both ships were exceptionally well armed, only a small proportion of the guns were mounted in the waist – the obvious location for heavier artillery pieces. The remains of the 800-ton *Sovereign* were discovered in Woolwich in 1912, and on examination it was found that she was clinker-built, although her hull was later rebuilt along carvel lines. The cutting of gunports would significantly weaken the hull structure of a clinker-built ship, while their introduction into a carvel-built hull would have far less impact. Her rebuilding would probably have taken place in 1509, when the vessel was refitted in Portsmouth.

Supporting evidence comes from the *Mary Rose*, laid down in the same year, 1509. An examination of her hull has suggested that unlike the *Sovereign* she was designed from the outset as a carvel-built warship. Moreover, the presence of three 'wales' suggests that she was built with strength in mind – these longitudinal supports helped to offset any structural weakness caused by the piercing of the hull with gunports. This permitted the mounting of guns on two decks – the level of the upper deck (which was in fact enclosed), and a lower purpose-built gundeck. While the *Sovereign* could be used as a merchant vessel if the need arose, the *Mary Rose* was built from the keel up as a weapon of war. This design focus suggests that by the accession of Henry VIII at the very latest, Tudor warships were capable of carrying substantial guns, and that ordnance had already become a major factor in warship construction.

THE *REGENT* AND THE *MARIE LA CORDELIERE*, BATTLE OFF BREST, 1512

The largest vessel of the Tudor navy until the appearance of the *Henri Grâce à Dieu*, the four-masted Regent was a floating symbol of Tudor power, richly decorated, and armed with no fewer than 225 guns, although almost all were handguns and swivel pieces. By the time Sir Thomas Knyvet sailed her into action against the French off Brest on 10 August 1512, she boasted an additional battery of heavy guns.

During the battle the powerful *Marie la Cordelière* became isolated from the rest of the French fleet and was surrounded by English warships. Captain Hervé de Porzmoguer held his own against all comers, but the *Regent* finally managed to grapple and board the French warship. As the two sides fought a fire broke out on the *Cordelière*, and the flames quickly spread to the *Regent*. Soon both warships were engulfed in flames, and both warships were lost, with tremendous loss of life. This scene recreates the moment when the two ships first clashed.

SPECIFICATIONS – *REGENT*

Type: A 'great ship' (carrack) originally known as the *Grace Dieu*. Built 1488.

Displacement: 1,000 tons.

Keel length: 140ft approx.

Beam: 45ft approx.

Armament: 180 guns (mostly swivel guns and handguns).

Crew (1512): 800 men (including 450 soldiers and 50 gunners).

Service notes: Participated in the battle off Brest, 1512, and was lost in action during the battle.

C

Purpose-built gun platforms

Various explanations have been proposed to explain the development of gunports, the most common being their invention by a Brest shipwright called Descharge, or their development at the behest of Henry VIII. Whatever the origin, their introduction marked a new phase in ship design. They became the symbol of the purpose-built warship – a vessel designed to employ naval artillery rather than simply to transport goods. At his accession in 1509, Henry VIII inherited a Tudor fleet of just six warships, a force which centred around the two carracks *Sovereign* and *Regent*. Of the remaining four, two were small 80-ton experimental vessels, described as 'galleys'. The ship *Michael* was a Scottish prize captured in 1488, while the 'carvel' *Mary and John* was a merchant vessel, the *Carvel of Ewe*, bought into service in 1487. Both had been dropped from the Navy Royal within two years. The two large warships were extensively rebuilt and redesigned to carry heavy ordnance, while Henry set about building up a fleet of purpose-built warships or warship conversions.

During the first three years of his reign Henry VIII ordered the construction of three major warships – the *Mary Rose*, *Peter Pomegranate* and *Great Bark* (I)[1] – all of which were three-masted carracks. In addition he purchased another eight vessels of 240–700 tons, the largest two of which were cochas from Genoa (the *Katherine Fortune* and the *Gabriel Royal*). All of these were transformed from merchant vessels into warships just in time for their participation in a war with France (1512–14). An engagement fought off Brest in April 1513 pitted these new ships against an equally well-armed French fleet, during which the value of heavy naval ordnance was clearly demonstrated. Clearly the process of conversion had not been as thorough as the king might have wished, as after the battle the English commander, Sir Edward Howard, reported that a recent purchase, the 300-ton *Christ*, was 'overladen with ordnance beside her heavy tops (castles) which are big enough for a ship of 800 or 900 tons'.

The largest addition to Henry VIII's fleet was the *Henri Grâce à Dieu* (nicknamed the 'Great Harry'), laid down in Woolwich in 1514. She was a

---

1 There were two ships called the *Great Bark* in the Tudor navy. The first was described as a 'ship' of 250 tons, and was built in 1512. She was eventually decommissioned and sold out of service in 1531. Rather confusingly, the *Great Galley*, built three years later in 1515 was actually an 800-ton galleass, which was rebuilt as a 500-ton 'ship' in 1542–43, and renamed as the *Great Bark* (See plate F specifications). These are referred to here respectively as the *Great Bark* (i) and the *Great Bark* (ii).

1,000-ton carrack, and her armament was listed as being no fewer than 112 guns. Although the majority of these were small swivel pieces or handguns, the comparison between her and the 1,000-ton *Regent* of 1488 is plain. While the latter carried a prodigious armament, only a handful of her guns were port pieces. By contrast the 'Great Harry' carried 43 heavy guns mounted on two main gundecks, and these included 20 modern bronze muzzle-loading artillery pieces. Whilst the *Regent* was designed as an assault ship intended primarily for boarding actions, Henry VIII's new flagship was a floating gun battery. She was also the largest carrack designed specifically as a warship – a vessel that impressed all those who saw her. Some 3,739 tons of timber were used in her construction (a total which includes three small tenders), together with 56 tons of iron.

The *Henri Grâce à Dieu* was described as being a four-masted 'great ship' (or large carrack), boasting a bonadventure mizzen – a fourth mast astern of her mizzen mast. She was also 'built loftie', with substantial forecastle and sterncastle structures, which would have made her as difficult to handle as she was imposing to look at. She was also almost certainly carvel-built. The last substantial clinker-built warship constructed for Henry VIII's Navy Royal was the *Great Galley*, built in 1515, and even she was rebuilt with a smooth carvel hull eight years later. Like the *Mary Rose* and other near-contemporary warships, Henry's namesake flagship had a squared-off stern, which not only simplified construction, but allowed the sterncastle to be more closely integrated into the hull of the ship. A comparison of engravings like the *Kraek* and the remains of the *Mary Rose* show just how far developed this process had become. The sterncastle of the *Mary Rose* sloped gradually upwards from the waist, and tapered slightly as it ran aft, in an effort to reduce the top-hamper (the weight of the superstructure) of the ship. According to its depictions in the *Anthony Roll*, and in common with all great ships or carracks in the Tudor fleet, the forecastle was higher and more imposing than the sterncastle. It therefore more closely resembled the design of earlier warships – even the *Grace Dieu* – than did the after part of the ship. However, evidence from the *Mary Rose* suggests that this feature was exaggerated in contemporary illustrations, and the sterncastle was the dominant feature of the Tudor warship's profile.

BELOW LEFT
The Grand Mistress, a 450-ton galleass built by Henry VIII in 1545, as depicted in the *Anthony Roll*. She was less than successful, and was reclassed as a ship four years later. (By permission of the Master & Fellows, Magdalene College, Cambridge)

BELOW
An English ship off Calais, depicted as part of a panoramic view of the port of c.1540 by Thomas Pettyt. The ship images from this view provide us with the earliest reliable evidence for the appearance of Tudor warships. (Cottonian Collection, National Science Museum)

The *Henri Grâce à Dieu*, the largest warship in Henry VIII's fleet, as depicted in the *Anthony Roll*. The document also contained a complete inventory of her crew, stores and armament. (By permission of the Master & Fellows, Magdalene College, Cambridge)

During the last three decades of Henry VIII's reign, the most important influence upon warship design was undoubtedly artillery. The desire to mount larger and more numerous pieces of ordnance meant that carrack designs had to be altered to cope with this demand. As the latest bronze guns could weigh almost 2 tons apiece, then clearly they had to be mounted as close to the waterline as possible. This meant not only piercing the hull with even more gunports, but also creating gundecks. Traditionally decks followed the line of the wale or sheer, which rose markedly towards the bow and stern. Obviously guns couldn't be mounted on a slope, and a level internal deck was considered impractical as for hull strength the gunports still had to follow the sheer line of the hull, placed between reinforcing wales. This meant that the gunports at either end would be too high. The solution was to break the deck in one or more places, effectively stepping the gundeck to correspond to the sheer of the hull.

In addition to the great ships or carracks of the Tudor fleet, Henry VIII also commissioned numerous smaller vessels, including galleys. Two 'prototype' galleasses were included in Henry VII's fleet, and although these appear to have been mothballed around 1525, Henry VIII clearly found these small oared vessels useful, as three more 80-ton galleys were commissioned in 1512, while over a dozen galleasses (all under 300 tons) were also added to the fleet during Henry's reign. The difference between the two was that while a galley was primarily an oared warship with auxiliary sails, a galleass combined the characteristics of a galley with a sailing ship – a curious hybrid designed to combine oar power with the all-round fighting ability of a sailing ship.

In 1515 the 500-ton *Great Galley* was built in Greenwich, which was actually a galleass similar to those found in the Mediterranean at the time (see New Vanguard 62: *Renaissance War Galley 1470–1590* for more information).

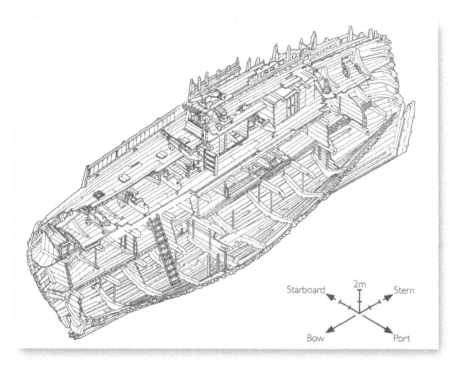

The rest of the galley fleet also followed French or Mediterranean lines, and was created largely as a means to counter the threat posed by a French galley fleet. In addition, 32 ships under 200 tons were listed between 1511 and 1546, of which 11 were prizes. Two barks, one prize hoy, 13 pinnaces (three of which were prizes) and 13 rowing barges were also included in the rolls of Henry VIII's Navy Royal. Pinnaces were single-masted vessels used as messenger boats and tenders, barges were used to transport supplies, while the barks and the hoy were simply differently rigged two- or three-masted versions of the fleet's smaller ships.

Building the *Mary Rose*

No English work on shipbuilding was published until the appearance of a collection of illustrated shipbuilder's notes in the later 16th century, a work now known as *Fragments of Ancient English Shipwrightry*. With no written evidence, our best source for understanding how the warships of Henry VIII's reign were built is the *Mary Rose*. The remains of this Tudor warship were raised from the waters of Portsmouth Harbour in 1982, and today these restored timbers are on display in a specially built museum. By taking a closer look at her construction, we might be able to understand a little more about how she and her sisters were built.

Like her contemporaries, the *Mary Rose* was built frame first (or 'skeleton built') – that is her keel was laid, a series of well-supported frames were attached to it that provided the shape of her hull, and then this structure was planked over using the carvel method. There is no evidence that she was ever converted from a clinker-built to a carvel-built ship. Her keel was 105ft long, constructed from three sections of elm joined together using scarf joints. The keel was strengthened by an oak keelson, which was also built in three sections. It appears that the majority of the frames were attached to the keel, but not to each other, or to other floor timbers – the exception being the stern transom frame. The frames themselves bulged out slightly before

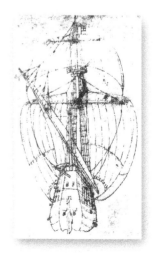

A model of the *Mary Rose*, based on the archaeological evidence produced during her excavation and recovery. If we contrast this with the *Anthony Roll* depiction of the vessel (page 27) we see that the artist of 1546 probably exaggerated the sweep and height of her quarterdeck structure, and even added extra guns to the main gundeck. (National Maritime Museum, Greenwich, London)

tapering towards the upper deck level, thus making the wale below the main gundeck the beamiest portion of the ship.

Longitudinal stringers (or braces) helped hold the frames in place, and oak knees (or brackets) attached to the frames were used to support the internal decks of the ship. The outward curve of the transom (rear) end of the sterncastle was supported by two horn timbers, and the whole transom frame was further supported by extra knees and braces. This method of construction is similar to that shown in the ship plans of Matthew Baker, dating from 1586, although this later manuscript described the construction of an Elizabethan race-built galleon.

A powerful Tudor warship off Calais, from a detail of Pettyt's panorama. The vessel shown here is similar in size to the *Mary Rose*, the *Peter*, the *Matthew* and the *Pauncy*. (Cottonian Collection, National Science Museum)

The *Mary Rose*'s hull was also strengthened during her life, with additional horizontal and diagonal braces, transom knees and riders being added to reinforce the stringers – presumably to help support the weight of additional ordnance. The vessel underwent two major refits, one in Portsmouth in 1527–28, the other in the Thames below London in 1536. In the process her displacement increased from 500 to 700 tons. The outer oak planking of the hull and transom stern was secured directly to the frames and stringers using wooden treenails. The average hull plank was around 4in (10cm) thick, and was further reinforced by the use of iron nails. The joints between the planks were then caulked, while reinforcing timber bands

(known as ribbands) protected additional caulking bands along the lower hull. The inside of the hull in the hold was also planked internally, thus forming a second skin below the waterline.

The internal and upper decks were constructed from deck planking attached to thick oaken beams, supported by knees attached to the frames. The *Mary Rose* was built with four deck spaces – a hold, an orlop deck, a main (or gundeck) and an upper deck. In addition, a fifth deck above the upper deck was built in the forecastle and sterncastle areas. The last three of these decks were designed to hold pieces of ordnance, and were strengthened accordingly with thicker knees and deck beams. A wale ran around the outer hull of the ship at the level of each of the three lower decks, thereby providing additional reinforcement to the structure. Like the hull planking itself, these three wales followed the sheer of the vessel, rising towards the bow and the stern. The wales also prevented the weakening of the hull by its piercing with gunports – seven ports being cut on either side of the vessel. The upper wale (at the level of the upper deck) also acted as an anchor for external fittings such as chainplates and other rigging fittings.

At the time of her sinking in 1546, the *Mary Rose* would have had a waterline length of 126ft, a beam of 38ft, a draught of 15ft, and the height of her sterncastle above the waterline was approximately 42ft. After construction in Portsmouth this impressive warship would have been fitted out by the addition of her masts and rigging, her internal fittings, and of course her *raison d'être* – the mounting of her guns.

The *Great Bark* (I) of 250 tons, built in 1512, was typical of the smaller warships in the fleet, and was used extensively for patrolling in the English Channel when the larger vessels were mothballed for the winter. (By permission of the Master & Fellows, Magdalene College, Cambridge)

OPERATIONAL HISTORY

Henry VII's navy
When Henry Tudor seized the throne in 1485, the majority of his royal warships were converted merchant vessels, two of which had only just been purchased by Richard III to help him counter the threat of a Tudor invasion.

D THE *MARY ROSE*, 1545

The first of Henry VIII's purpose-built warships, the *Mary Rose* – named after Henry's sister – was built in Portsmouth in 1509. She was designed to carry heavy ordnance, and was therefore carvel-built, which permitted her hull to be pierced with gunports. The effectiveness of her firepower was demonstrated in her first battle, fought off Brest in 1513. She dismasted the French flagship and sent her scurrying back into port, followed by the bulk of the enemy fleet. She then saw service in the war against Scotland (1514). She was also known as a fast sailing ship – Admiral Sir Edward Howard once claimed that no 100-ton ship in the fleet could outsail the *Mary Rose*. The vessel underwent a major refit in 1536, when even more heavy guns were added, and her decks strengthened to take the extra weight. Inset is a bronze 'bastard' culverin reconstructed from one found on the wreck.

The *Mary Rose* formed part of the Tudor fleet that opposed the French at the battle off Portsmouth; on 18 July 1545 she sailed out to give battle. However, a sudden gust of wind caused her to heel over, and water poured into her lower gunports, which her undisciplined crew had failed to close. She sank within minutes, taking most of her 700-man crew down with her.

The wreck of the *Mary Rose* was rediscovered in 1970, and a major underwater archaeological operation was launched to investigate it, and to recover the ship's contents. In 1982 this operation culminated in the raising of the remains of her hull, and she now forms part of a purpose-built display at the Mary Rose Trust's museum in Portsmouth.

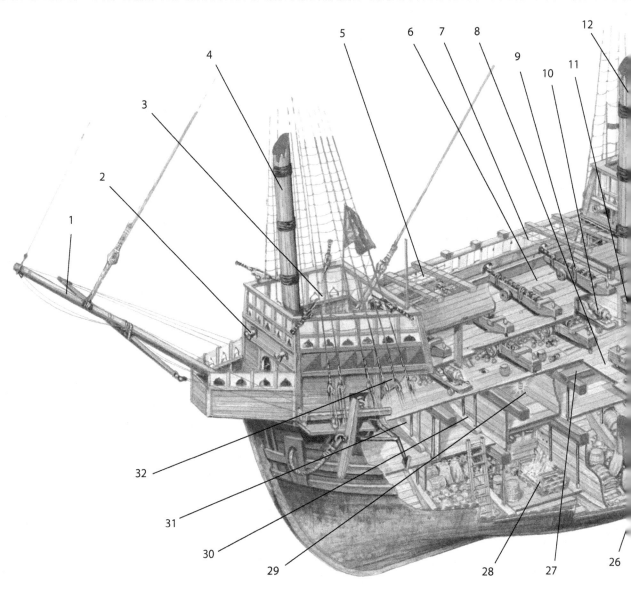

SPECIFICATIONS – *MARY ROSE*

Type: A 'great ship' (carrack). Built 1509 (Portsmouth).

Displacement: 500 tons.*

Keel length: 105ft

Beam: 38ft

Armament: 60 guns (44 heavy, the rest swivel guns).

Crew (1512): 400 men (including 200 soldiers and 20 gunners).

Service notes: Rebuilt 1536. Participated in the battle off Brest (1513) and the battle off Portsmouth (1545). She capsized and sank during the latter battle.

* 700 tons after her 1536 refit.

KEY

1 Bowsprit
2 Bow chasers (sakers)
3 Forecastle
4 Foremast
5 Anti-boarding netting
6 Waist
7 Blinds (designed to screen the crew)
8 Main gundeck
9 Port piece
10 Demi culverin
11 Companionway access to the main deck
12 Mainmast
13 Barber surgeon's cabin
14 Archery port
15 Mizzen mast
16 Carpenter's cabin
17 Quarterdeck
18 Bonadventure mizzen
19 Admiral's cabin
20 Captain's cabin
21 Rudder
22 Beer and spirit store
23 Hold
24 Ship's stores
25 Ballast
26 Main pump
27 Orlop deck
28 Galley
29 Powder magazine
30 Boatswain's store
31 Anchor cabin
32 Pilot's cabin

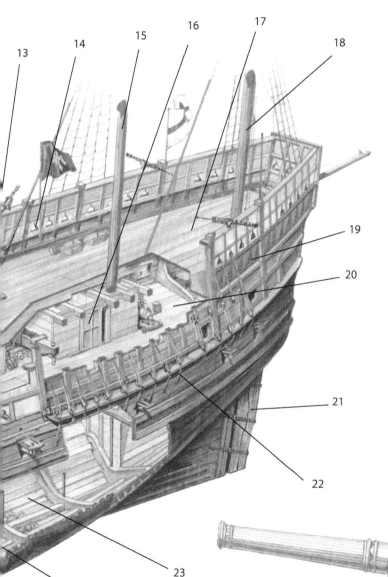

A well-armed Tudor warship off Calais, taken from a detail of Pettyt's panorama. It has been suggested that the vessel depicted could be the *Sweepstake*, of 300 tons. (Cottonian Collection, National Science Museum)

As a deterrent the fleet had proved highly unsuccessful, largely because its only admiral, Sir Edward Woodville, had defected to Henry Tudor two years previously, taking two of the ships (the *Fawkon* and the *Trinity*) with him, filled with royal gold snatched from the Tower of London. Woodville retained his position as Admiral of the Narrows and the Channel, and a new group of carefully selected ship captains helped ensure the loyalty of the Navy Royal to the new Tudor regime.

Richard III's Navy Royal consisted of eight warships, seven of which were carracks, and the *Nickolas of London*, which was described as a 'great ship'. Thomas Rodgers, the Yorkist Keeper of the King's Ships, managed to keep his job when Henry VII took the throne that August, and he duly presented his new monarch with a detailed account of the fleet anchored in the River Thames off the Tower of London. It didn't make particularly good reading, as many of the vessels on the list were either old or in poor repair. Three of these ships, the *Grace Dieu* (or *Grace de Dieu*), the *Mary of the Tower* and the *Governor*, were moved to a new anchorage in the River Hamble near Southampton, where they were mothballed. The *Governor* was sold to London merchants the following year. The *Grace Dieu* was 12 years old, and although she had been refitted during her service life she was deemed obsolete. In 1488 the decision was made to break her up, and use her timbers and fittings for the construction of a new royal vessel, the *Sovereign*.

The stoutly built *Nickolas of London* had recently been purchased by Richard III for 100 Marks, and was undergoing conversion into a warship when the king died at Bosworth in August 1485. Unsure of his fiscal position, her new royal owner, Henry VII, ordered the work stopped and the vessel sold before costs could escalate. He also disposed of two of his carracks. The converted merchantman *Fawkon* was sold to London merchants, while the *Martin Garcia* was gifted to Sir Richard Guildeford, the Master of the Ordnance. The latter was a Portuguese carrack that had been bought into royal service by the last Lancastrian king, Henry VI, in 1470, and judging by the accounts she was in an advanced state of decay by the time she left royal service. That left Henry VII with a Navy Royal of just five warships, only two of which, the *Bonadventure* and the *Trinity*, were fit for service.

The carrack *Bonadventure* (formerly known as the *Bark of Southampton*) was bought into service in 1483, so we can presume she was in reasonably good condition. Although Sir Edward Woodville's flagship *Trinity* was older, having been purchased in 1478, the fact that she remained in royal service for two decades suggests that the carrack was a well-founded vessel. As for the mothballed *Mary of the Tower*, after being moved from the Hamble to nearby Burlesdon she remained there for less than a year before she was leased to private London owners for a mercantile voyage to the Mediterranean. On her return in the summer of 1487 she was taken to Greenwich, where she was mothballed once again. She remained there for another nine years, before being sold out of service in 1496.

Given his general policy of fiscal prudence, what Henry VII did next seemed somewhat out of character. In early 1486 he ordered Sir Richard Guildeford and Thomas Rodgers to draw up plans for the building of two purpose-built great ships, the first royal vessels to be designed from the keel up as warships since the laying down of the original *Grace Dieu* on the orders of Henry V in 1418. Guildeford was ordered to supervise the building of the first of these, also called the *Grace Dieu*, on Reding Creek, which flowed into the River Rother a few miles above Rye, on the Sussex coast. In 1489, while the 450-ton vessel was being fitted out, she was re-named the *Regent*. The second great ship was even larger. The building of the 800-ton *Trinity Sovereign* in Southampton was supervised by Sir Reginald Bray, and like her counterpart she entered service in 1489, at which point her name was shortened to *Sovereign*.

Henry VIII, with the *Mary Rose* in the background. This depiction is from a Royal Mail stamp, brought out to commemorate the raising of the *Mary Rose* in 1982. (Stratford Archive)

Clearly Henry had decided to strengthen his navy, which he considered his first line of defence against an invasion – the like of which he had launched against Richard III's kingdom. These two prestigious warships were designed as much as a warning to potential claimants to the throne as they were new acquisitions to his fleet in their own right. In 1487 Henry purchased another vessel, the 180-ton *Carvel of Ewe*, the carvel having been hired by Sir Edward Woodville to augment his invasion fleet two years before. This brought the active fleet strength up to three warships. The fleet was further strengthened by two Scottish prizes, the *Michael*, captured in 1488, and the *Margaret*, which was taken as a prize two years later. The *Margaret* was disposed of before 1509, but the *Michael* – a vessel of unknown size – remained in service until 1513.

After building his two great ships, Henry VII only made two subsequent additions to the fleet. Upon realizing the potential of the galley fleet operated by the French, Henry attempted his own experiment with oared warships. In 1497 he commissioned two prototype galleasses – 80-ton three-masted vessels which were built along conventional lines, but which were fitted with rowing ports and oars. It has been suggested that the design was copied from Venetian trading galleasses which first put in to English ports during Henry's reign. Although we don't know where the *Mary Fortune* was built, her sister ship the *Sweepstake* was constructed in Portsmouth – the first royal warship to be built there. When Henry VII died in April 1509, this small handful of ships constituted the entire Navy Royal. Apart from the two galleasses, the rest were all over 20 years old at a time when the life of a wooden vessel was set at around a quarter of a century. It was hardly an inspiring legacy for the young Henry VIII.

BELOW

The *Anne Gallant*, the second Tudor ship to hold that name, was a 450-ton galleass, built in 1545. This *Anthony Roll* depiction shows her as a sleek four-masted vessel. (By permission of the Master & Fellows, Magdalene College, Cambridge)

BOTTOM

The *Roseslip* (or *Rose Slyp*) was a small 20-ton rowing barge, one of 14 built in 1546. They were primarily used as fleet tenders. However, in this *Anthony Roll* depiction the artist has shown a much larger warship, similar to the 160-ton *Tiger*, which was built at the same time. (By permission of the Master & Fellows, Magdalene College, Cambridge)

Henry VIII's navy

The Navy Royal inherited by Henry VIII on his accession consisted of just six warships, only two of which – the *Regent* (1,000 tons) and *Sovereign* (800 tons) – displaced more than 200 tons. His father had relied on hired merchant vessels to augment his fleet in time of war, but the young Henry had other plans. While hired vessels were still an important part of his naval programme, the English king also intended to build up the strength of his own permanent navy. He began with the commissioning of two purpose-built warships – the *Mary Rose* (500 tons) and the *Peter Pomegranate* (450 tons), both of which were laid down in Portsmouth in 1509. Both were designed to carry artillery, although it wasn't until the vessels were rebuilt in 1536 that their timbers allowed the deployment of a full suite of heavy bronze ordnance. This pair constituted the first modern warships in the fleet.

For the next five years Henry added to the fleet by purchasing larger vessels overseas, and building smaller ones (including a squadron of galleys) at home. None of these vessels were particularly memorable or enjoyed as much longevity as his two purpose-built warships, but together they contributed to a fivefold increase in the size of the fleet within half a decade. The bulk of this naval expansion took place in 1512, when a fresh war with France and her Scottish ally found the Navy Royal ill-equipped to protect the English coastline, let alone do very much else.

The war began in December 1511, but little happened until the following spring. Fortunately there was only one major naval engagement during the war, fought off Brest in August 1512. By that stage Henry had built up his Navy Royal sufficiently, and had supported it with a large fleet of hired armed merchantmen. The battle itself was inconclusive (although *Regent* was lost), but it clearly demonstrated the efficacy of arming warships with heavy ordnance. Consequently, Henry placed an even greater emphasis on the arming of his fleet with artillery.

Finally, in 1514, Henry was ready for his largest naval challenge yet. He commissioned the *Henri Grâce à Dieu*, a 1,000-ton great ship that was designed to embody the power and majesty of the English state. Although it was claimed that the 'Great Harry' carried up to 112 guns, only 51 of them were considered to be large pieces, augmented by around 29 small swivel guns. The remaining pieces were handguns. She also carried a complement of 260 sailors and 400 soldiers. While she might have looked prestigious, she was not particularly successful as a warship. For a start, she

The *Mary Rose*, as shown in the *Anthony Roll*. (By permission of the Master & Fellows, Magdalene College, Cambridge)

would have drawn too much water to enter Dover or Calais, which means that the well-known depiction of Henry's embarkation at Dover in 1520 when he sailed to meet the French king Francis I at 'The Field of the Cloth of Gold' is fanciful – a statement in art rather than a depiction of maritime reality. The ineffectiveness of the floating leviathan is borne out by the documentary evidence, which suggests that the 'Great Harry' took no part in the transport of the English king to the Continent.

The meeting between the two monarchs did little to diffuse the tension between the two countries, and in November 1521 Henry signed a secret treaty with the Holy Roman Emperor Charles V, which committed him to a new war with France. Hostilities began the following June, and a month later the English fleet landed an army on the Brittany coast, which captured and sacked Morlaix. Lacking the strength to attack Brest, Sir William Fitzwilliam defeated a small French squadron off Le Treport near Dieppe, on the Normandy coast, and then returned to his winter anchorage in the River Thames. The Tudor (and Stuart) custom was to keep the bulk of the fleet in port during winter, leaving a small 'Winter Guard' to patrol the coasts. The following year the fleet achieved even less, and in January 1524 a French squadron captured two ships of the Winter Guard as they lay off Sandwich, one of which was the *Kateryn Galley* (80 tons). Honour was saved when two French barks were captured the following month. The war fizzled out later that year, and a peace treaty was duly signed in early 1525 following the capture of Francis I at the battle of Pavia.

In the decade between the building of the *Henri Grâce à Dieu* and the end of this latest French war the fleet had grown by 17 ships, four of which were prizes. The 'Great Harry' spent the whole war mothballed at Northfleet (by Gravesend, on the River Thames), which only served to highlight the impracticality of her design. However, the *Mary Rose* and the *Peter*

27

An *Anthony Roll* depiction of the *Peter Pomegranate* (known simply as the *Peter* from 1536). She was a near-sister of the *Mary Rose*, and like her she was fully refurbished to accommodate a heavier suite of ordnance. (By permission of the Master & Fellows, Magdalene College, Cambridge)

Pomegranate both played an active part in the fleet, as did Henry's later great ships, the *Gabriel Royal* (700 tons), the *Great Barbara* (400 tons) and the *Great Galley*, a magnificent galleass of 800 tons which was built in Greenwich in 1515, and rebuilt as a 500-ton sailing ship in 1524. For the most part these large ships were mothballed during the winter, leaving the smaller ships of the fleet to maintain the winter patrol.

The last two decades of Henry's reign saw a continuation of his policy of building up the fleet using a combination of a few large, prestigious warships, supported by a greater number of smaller vessels. In effect he created a main battle fleet, supported by a host of patrol vessels, galleys for inshore work and support vessels to accompany the main fleet when it sailed into action. These smaller vessels were used to escort fishing fleets and merchantmen, to hunt pirates and to provide an early warning of any hostile activity in the English Channel, the Irish Sea or the North Sea.

The *Unicorn* was a French-built galleass which was employed in Scottish service. She was captured in the Firth of Forth in 1544, then added to the strength of the Tudor fleet. Three years after her depiction in the *Anthony Roll* she was rebuilt as a sailing warship. (By permission of the Master & Fellows, Magdalene College, Cambridge)

This was not a period that saw as rapid a naval expansion as before, but it did see an extensive rebuilding of the older ships in the fleet. By 1528 the oldest remaining ship was the *Mary Rose* (19 years old), and a refit that year prolonged her active life for another seven years, although she spent the whole time in mothballs. She was completely rebuilt in 1536–38, as was the *Peter Pomegranate* and the 'Great Harry'. However, the late 1530s was a time of growing international tension following Henry's break with the Catholic Church, and with the Pope calling for a crusade against England, Henry wanted to make sure his fleet was ready to meet any challenge. In addition to improving his older ships, Henry embarked on another rapid expansion of the fleet, commissioning the building of nine new vessels between 1539 and 1544, and the purchase of four more.

In 1543 the bulk of the fleet sailed north to support operations against the Scots, and in 1544 they actively supported the English army when it invaded Scotland. The fleet harassed shipping in the Firth of Forth and participated in the burning of Leith before hurrying south to meet the new threat posed by the French, who had declared war on England late the previous year. The big attack finally came in July 1545, when the French attacked the English fleet in what became known as the battle of Portsmouth. This engagement will be described later, but the most spectacular outcome was the capsize of the *Mary Rose*, in full view of the king, who was watching from the shore. The venerable Tudor warship sank in minutes, taking most of her 700-man crew down with her. Henry's loss was our gain, for the wreck of the *Mary Rose* was rediscovered and excavated during the early 1980s, and she now forms the centrepiece of a dedicated museum in Portsmouth.

Henry died just two years later, leaving his son, Edward VI, with a Navy Royal that was both substantial and modern. It consisted of 57 warships, of which 11 were described as great ships, and 15 more as galleasses or galleys. The tiny fleet Henry inherited from his father had been a fleet designed to fight boarding actions. The fleet he left his own son was one built around the naval gun – a force which would be seen as the precursor of the Royal Naval battle

An English warship sailing with the wind on her beam, by Pettyt. From this aspect the decoration around her stern and quarterdeck is clearly visible. (Cottonian Collection, National Science Museum)

This detail of *Henry VIII's Embarkation for France* shows a group of large Tudor warships taking on men and stores. Although this scene was painted long after the event, the artist seems to have captured the general appearance of Tudor warships of Henry VIII's reign. It is taken from a reproduction of the original painting in Hampton Court Palace. (Stratford Archive)

fleet of 'the age of fighting sail'. During his reign the fleet had been transformed by the introduction of naval ordnance, and royal gun foundries had been created to supply Henry's ships with the latest types of bronze ordnance.

Henry's naval achievement went further than this. During his reign the administration of the fleet was developed, and a dedicated body of officials now saw to its wellbeing and maintenance. Dockyards had been built, dry docks constructed and shipyards expanded, while all the time the skills of English shipbuilders had been challenged and developed, until they could produce vessels worthy of Henry's approval. Just over a decade later this magnificent fleet would be gifted to his daughter Elizabeth, and under her guidance it would develop into a force capable of defeating the greatest naval power in renaissance Europe.

ARMAMENT AND GUNNERY

Armament

The easiest way to demonstrate the transformation that the Tudor navy went through during the reigns of the first two Tudor monarchs is to compare the armament of two major warships, one from each end of the period.

In 1485 the *Grace Dieu* carried just 21 guns, all handguns capable of being rested on the gunwale of the ship. Ten years later in 1495 an inventory of the *Sovereign* lists no fewer than 140 guns, of which all but 31 were serpentines (handguns). The remainder (20 in the waist and 11 more below the sterncastle)

THE *SALAMANDER* AND THE *SWALLOW*, 1546

Like her near-sister the *Unicorn*, the *Salamander* was captured from the Scots in the Firth of Forth in 1544, and was added to the strength of Henry VIII's Navy Royal. By the time of her depiction in the *Anthony Roll* two years later, all trace of her oars had disappeared, although she still possessed the graceful lines associated with a fast oared warship. By contrast the *Swallow* was an English-built galleass, a class of ship with which Henry VIII was fascinated. She participated in the battle off Portsmouth, then went on to serve in Elizabeth I's navy. Altogether she was rated as a far more effective fighting warship than the French-built *Salamander*.

SPECIFICATIONS – *SALAMANDER*

Type: A galleass, built in France (1537), and captured from the Scots in 1544.

Displacement: 300 tons.

Keel length: 80ft approx.

Beam: 22ft approx.

Armament: 36 guns (16 heavy, the rest swivel guns).

Crew (1512): 140 men (including 130 soldiers and 30 gunners).

Service notes: Reclassified as a ship in 1549, and rebuilt as a 'galleon' (1549). Sold in 1603.

SPECIFICATIONS – *SWALLOW*

Type: A galleass, built in 1544.

Displacement: 300 tons.

Keel length: 80ft approx.

Beam: 22ft approx.

Armament: 38 guns (21 heavy, the rest swivel guns).

Crew (1512): 400 men (including 180 soldiers and 20 gunners).

Service notes: Condemned in 1559.

were stone guns – small pieces resembling mini mortars, capable of firing roundshot carved from stone. The shot fragmented on impact, and were considered excellent anti-personnel weapons – the forerunner of grapeshot canisters. In other words, while the *Grace Dieu* relied on archers for her firepower, the *Sovereign* was protected by handgunners, augmented by a small battery of guns firing anti-personnel shot.

By the time Henry VIII came to the throne the composition had changed again. In 1509 the *Sovereign* was armed with: 4 whole curtows of bronze; 3 half-curtows of brass; 2 falcons of brass; 7 great pieces of iron; 4 serpentines of brass; 42 serpentines of iron (great and small); 4 slings of iron; 2 stone guns for the top; and one culverin without a stock. Of the 69 guns listed, the serpentines were essentially handguns, while the slings were small swivel guns. The falcons were very light bronze pieces, of limited use on board a ship. Therefore, discounting the culverin without a carriage, her armament consisted of 14 heavy guns, of which just over half were muzzle-loading pieces cast in bronze. The great pieces (also known as port pieces or murderers) were substantial wrought-iron guns, built up using iron staves and iron hoops, with a limited range and velocity. However, a combination of these pieces and the more modern bronze guns (curtows and half-curtows) meant that the *Sovereign* possessed an impressive level of firepower for her day – a period when ships were still not pierced with gunports, and if they were embarked at all heavy guns were carried on the open deck. A comparison of these two

List of ordnance returned to the Tower of London after voyage, c.1495		
Gun type	Weight of shot (lb)	Weight of powder (lb)
Bombardelle	263	60
Curtow	100	40
Demi-Curtow	40	27
Serpentine	6	7
Falcon	1 (lead)	1

List of artillery required by army, 1513		
Gun type	Weight of shot (lb)	Weight of powder (lb)
Bombard	260	80
Curtow	60	40
Culverin	20	22
Minion	8	8
Pot Gun	4 (stone)	40

Armament of Henry VIII's major warships, c.1512[1]						
Gun type	Henri Grâce à Dieu (1,000 tons)	Great Elizabeth (900 tons)	Gabriel Royal (700 tons)	Katherine Fortileza (700 tons)	Mary Rose (500 tons)	Peter Pomegranate (450 tons)
Culverins	2	–	2	–	–	–
Curtows	1	–	1	1	5	–
Murderers	18	8	3	14	6	11
Stone guns	24	29	9	13	26	6
Falcons	6	–	14	2	5	2
Slings	1	6	2	6	2	3
Cast guns	–	–	–	–	2	–
Others	5	–	–	–	–	–

1 These totals exclude both the lighter swivel guns and handguns listed in the inventories of these ships.

inventories with a later Tudor list suggests that the curtow and half-curtow were early prototypes of the cannon and demi-cannon (see below).

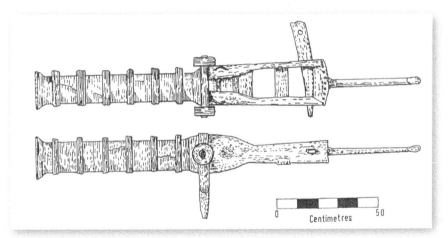

The weapons described above were essentially the armament of Henry VIII's navy when it embarked on its first war with France in 1512, the first naval campaign fought by the Navy Royal where gunpowder weapons played a major part. However, the intention was to fire the guns once or at most twice, immediately before boarding an enemy ship. There was no intention to use the pieces as a means of battering an enemy vessel from long range – the very composition of the ordnance carried on the *Sovereign* showed that the emphasis was on close-range anti-personnel fire. This emphasis would change.

The earliest evidence we have for the distribution of guns on an early Tudor warship dates from 1496, when a detailed account of the location of ordnance was provided for the *Sovereign*. (Drawing by author)

If we look at the armament of some of the ships of the Navy Royal at the end of Henry VIII's reign we can see that the number of large bronze guns increased dramatically. Take the *Mary Rose* as an example – she carried five large bronze pieces in 1509, but by 1545 she was rearmed with 13 substantial bronze guns. This upgunning represents a considerable investment by Henry VIII, who embraced the new gun founding technologies with a passion. Comparing the armament of his warships at the start and the end of his reign reveals two very obvious developments. The first was the increase in gun size – a greater reliance on large pieces rather than on small swivel guns and hand-held weapons. The second was the steady increase in the number and quality of bronze guns carried on board the ships of his Navy Royal.

As gun founding technology improved, and the efficiency of these new bronze guns was demonstrated, Henry began augmenting the armament of his major warships with bronze guns. By the 1540s these new weapons outnumbered the older large wrought-iron pieces that had hitherto been the principal heavy armament of the fleet. Towards the end of his reign the first reliable cast-iron guns began to appear, first on board armed merchantmen, and then – as a result of the invasion scare of 1545 – on board Henrician warships. Nevertheless, the older wrought-iron pieces remained in use

A wrought-iron breech-loading swivel gun, of a kind which was commonly found on vessels of this period (see Plate F inset). In Tudor inventories these weapons were called 'slings' or 'bases'. The yoke – resembling the rowlock on a rowing boat – was slotted into a hole on the ship's rail. A bag of shot would be inserted in the breech, followed by the powder chamber (not shown here), and the piece would then be ready to fire. (Drawing by author)

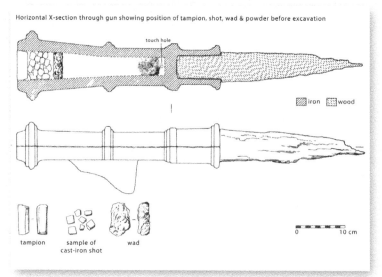

Horizontal X-section through gun showing position of tampion, shot, wad & powder before excavation

touch hole

iron   wood

0   10 cm

tampion   sample of   wad
            cast-iron shot

throughout his reign, and the guns recovered from the *Mary Rose* clearly demonstrate that these weapons remained a useful and cost-effective supplement to more modern pieces. Finally, the number of swivel guns and other small pieces actually increased, although their proportion compared to the heavier guns decreased. It was all part of the same general trend towards increasing the power and effectiveness of shipborne artillery.

It is worth looking briefly at the different forms of gun design used by Henry's navy.

The *Anthony Roll* inventory shows that most Tudor warships carried numerous 'hailshot pieces', which were essentially large anti-personnel weapons, filled with small scraps of iron. It resembled an over-sized handgun, and the flange on the underside of the barrel was hooked over the ship's rail to absorb the recoil when the piece was fired. (Mary Rose Trust)

Wrought-iron breech-loading pieces

The technology involved in forging wrought-iron guns was little different from that used by contemporary blacksmiths. This meant these weapons were relatively easy to produce, and their production didn't involve the Royal Exchequer in a large outlay for the hire of specialist gun founders or expensive raw materials. Suitable iron was readily available, and this form of gun construction had been practiced for more than a century. Strips of iron were grouped around a wooden former to create the barrel, and then a series of wrought-iron rings were heat-shrunk over this core, creating a series of reinforcers that bound the weapon together. The result was a long wrought-iron tube that resembled a long wooden barrel (hence this is where the ordnance term 'barrel' probably first had its origins).

These guns were breech-loading pieces, the powder chamber being constructed as a separate piece, which was withdrawn completely from the

Armament of Henry VIII's major warships, c.1545[1]

Gun type	Mary Rose (500 tons)	Peter Pomegranate (450 tons)	Great Galley (500 tons)	Small Galley (400 tons)	Sweepstake (300 tons)	Jennet (200 tons)
Cannons	–	2	5	2	–	–
Demi-cannons	4	2	–	6	–	–
Culverins	2	1	–	–	–	–
Demi-culverins	2	–	2	6	–	–
Sakers	5	5	4	2	2	1
Falcons	2	–	2	–	3	1
Port pieces	9	10	12	10	9	6
Fowlers	6	15	–	–	2	4
Bases	–	–	50	30	8	6
Slings	6	4	2	7	4	7
Quarter slings	60	52	10	10	16	21

1 The armament of these ships changed regularly – these figures reflect a 'snapshot' of their armament, listed in an inventory in 1545. This time the figures include all swivel guns (listed as 'slings, bases and quarter slings'). By this stage handguns were no longer listed alongside the artillery armament of the ships.

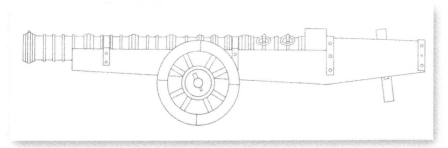

This wrought-iron breech-loading gun – a 'port piece' – was recovered from the wreck of the *Mary Rose*, where it formed part of the armament of the lower gundeck. The piece was mounted on a wooden 'sled' carriage, which in turn was mounted on two wooden wheels. The wooden post at the back could be used to elevate the piece. (Drawing by Rudi Roth, author's collection)

gun while the piece was being loaded. In almost all cases the barrel and the chamber were sunk into a wooden bed, and when it was fitted into place the chamber would be locked in place with an iron wedge. The drawback of this type of weapon was that there was considerable gas leakage from the join between the barrel and the chamber when the piece was fired. This reduced the velocity of the projectile and lessened its destructive power. However, as long as there was at least one spare chamber per gun, these weapons could be reloaded comparatively quickly and with little fuss. These weapons were also perfectly good at doing what was usually expected of them – delivering effective fire at close range, probably as part of a broadside fired immediately before the ship came alongside an enemy and initiated a boarding action. Typical guns of this type were the murderers or port pieces (both similar to the Spanish *bombardetta*), which remained mainstays of the Tudor naval arsenal throughout Henry VIII's reign. These also included stone guns – low-velocity pieces designed to fire stone shot at a low velocity. Most swivel guns (often called slings or 'bases' – similar to the Spanish *verso*) were also constructed in roughly the same way.

Bronze muzzle-loading pieces

Although ordnance had been cast from bronze since the mid-14th century, it was not until the first decade of the 16th century that the English truly embraced this new technology. Henry VIII imported skilled gun founders from Italy – Arcani (Arcanus) of Cesena and Jeronimo (Jeronimus) of Milan were both taken into the royal employ, and produced bronze guns for the Navy Royal. There was also a group of domestic gun founders who rose to the challenge – most notably Humphrey Walker, who operated in the Tower of London during the first decade of Henry's reign, and then the brothers John and Robert Owen, who set up their own gun foundry in Houndsditch, a mile to the north. However, the majority of the bronze guns used on board Henry VIII's warships were imported, most being supplied by the gun founder Hans Poppenruyter of Malines, in Flanders.

The problem with large bronze guns was their weight – the barrels were much more heavily reinforced than bronze guns of the same calibre produced in later centuries. The other problem was the expense – they cost three times the price of a wrought-iron or cast-iron piece of comparable size and weight. Still, these guns made up for this high cost in their performance, and gave Henry's warships the ability to damage enemy vessels at a far greater range than before. They were also a prestigious addition to the fleet, and proved to observers that the Navy Royal was a modern and well-equipped force. The nature of bronze guns changed very slightly during Henry's reign, as reflected in the comparison between the fleet armament in 1512 and 1545. While the original pieces were divided into the longer culverins and the shorter but

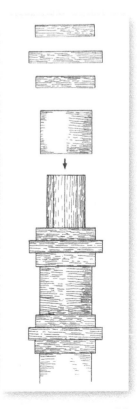

The construction of a wrought-iron breech-loading gun was relatively simple: a series of iron staves with slightly bevelled edges was formed into a hollow tube, the edges helping the strips form a circle. Then a series of wrought-iron rings of varying thicknesses and widths were heat-shrunk around the staves, thus forming a tube capable of withstanding the pressure of a gunpowder explosion. (Drawing by author)

Major additions to Henry VIII's Navy Royal, 1509–47

Date	Vessel	Type	Tonnage	Notes	Service ended
1509 (B)	Mary Rose	Ship	500 tons	Rebuilt 1536 (as 700-ton vessel). 60 guns	1545
1510 (B)	Peter Pomegranate	Ship	450 tons	Renamed Peter, 1536	60 guns
1512 (P)	Christ	Ship	300 tons		Captured by Turks, 1515
1512 (P)	Maria de Larreto	Carrack	800 tons	Captured from Genoese	Returned to Genoa, 1514
1512 (P)	Katherine Fortune	Carrack	550 tons	Sometimes known as Katherine Fortileza. Purchased from Genoa	Wrecked, 1521
1512 (P)	Gabriel Royal	Carrack	700 tons	Purchased from Genoa	1526
1512 (P)	John Baptist	Ship	400 tons	Sometimes known as Ship of John Hopton	Wrecked, 1534
1512 (P)	Mary George	Ship	250 tons	22 guns	1526
1512 (P)	Mary James	Ship	240 tons	Rebuilt 1524	1529
1512 (P)	Great Nicholas	Ship	400 tons		1522
1512 (B)	Great Bark	Ship	250 tons		1531
1513 (P)	Great Barbara	Carrack	400 tons		1524
1514 (B)	Henri Grâce à Dieu	Ship	1,000 tons	80 guns. Renamed Edward, 1547	Destroyed by fire, 1553
1514 (P)	Great Elizabeth	Ship	900 tons	Purchased from Lubeck	Wrecked, 1514
1515 (B)	Great Galley	Galleass	500 tons	Rebuilt 1523, then again in 1542 as a ship. Renamed Great Bark (II) in 1543	1562
1517 (P)	Mary Gloria	Ship	300 tons		1522
1530 (U)	Trinity Henry	Ship	250 tons	64 guns	1558
1535 (B)	Sweepstake	Ship	300 tons	84 guns	1559
1539 (B)	Matthew	Ship	600 tons	131 guns	1558
1543 (B)	Pauncy	Ship	450 tons	97 guns	1558
1544 (P)	Jesus of Lubeck	Ship	700 tons	70 guns. Purchased from Lubeck	Captured by Spanish, 1568
1544 (P)	Marryan	Ship	500 tons	63 guns. Purchased from Hamburg	1551
1544 (P)	Struce	Ship	450 tons	39 guns. Purchased from Hamburg	1552
1544 (P)	Mary Hambro	Ship	400 tons	70 guns. Purchased from Hamburg	1558
1544 (C)	Unicorn	Galleass	250 tons	36 guns. French galleass, captured from Scots. Rebuilt as a ship, 1549	1552
1544 (C)	Salamander	Galleass	300 tons	49 guns. French galleass, captured from Scots. Rebuilt as a ship, 1549	1559
1545 (P)	Christopher of Bream	Ship	400 tons	53 guns. Purchased from Danzig. Renamed Christopher (II), 1548	1556
1546 (B)	Hart	Galleass	300 tons	Rebuilt as a ship by 1549	1568
1546 (P)	Antelope	Galleass	300 tons	Rebuilt as a ship by 1549	Destroyed by fire, 1649

(B) = Built   (P) = Purchased   (C) = Captured   (U) = Origin unknown

Vessels of 200 tons or less:

Unless noted otherwise, the last date represents the year in which the ship was last mentioned in the official records. Pinnaces, barks, hoys and rowing barges have not been included in this list as neither group were designed to function as operational warships.

Ships

1511 (C) *Jennet Prywin* (70 tons). Formerly *Andrew Barton*. Captured from Scots. 1514

1511 (C) *Lion* (120 tons, 36 guns). Captured from Scots. 1513

1512 (B) *Anne Gallant* (140 tons). Wrecked 1518

1512 (B) *Dragon* (100 tons). 1514

1512 (P) *Lizard* (120 tons). 1522

1512 (U) *Barbara of Greenwich* (140 tons). 1514

1513 (P) *Henry Hampton* (120 tons). 1521

1513 (U) *Mary Imperial* (100 tons). 1525

1517 (U) *Less Bark* (180 tons). Renamed *Small Bark*, 1536. 1552

1518 (B) *Katherine Bark* (100 tons). 1525

1519 (U) *Trinity Henry* (80 tons). 1525

1522 (U) *Madeleine of Deptford* (120 tons). 1525

1523 (U) *John of Greenwich* (50 tons). 1530

1523 (B) *Primrose* (160 tons). Rebuilt as 240-ton vessel in 1538. Sold 1555

1523 (B) *Minion* (160 tons). Rebuilt as 300-ton vessel in 1536. Given away 1549

1524 (B) *Mary Guildford* (160 tons). 1539

1535 (B) *Mary Willoughby* (140 tons). Captured by Scots, 1536, recaptured 1547

1543 (C) *Artigo* (140 tons). Captured from the French. Sold 1547

1545 (C) *Mary Thomas* (100 tons). Captured from the French. 1546

1545 (C) *Mary James* (120 tons). Captured from the French. 1546

1545 (C) *Mary Odierne* (70 tons). Captured from the French. 1545

1545 (C) *Trinity* (80 tons) Captured from the French. 1545

1545 (C) *Sacrett* (160 tons) Captured from the French. Condemned 1559

Galleys and Galleasses

1512 (B) *Henry Galley* (80 tons). Sunk 1513

1512 (U) *Rose Galley* (80 tons). 1521

1513 (U) *Kateryn Galley* (80 tons). 1527

1536 (B) *Lion* (140 tons – galleass). Listed as a ship from 1549. 1552

1539 (B) *Jennet* (180 tons – galleass). Listed as a ship from 1549. 1589

1542 (B) *Dragon* (140 tons – galleass). Listed as a ship from 1549. 1552

1543 (B) *Galley Subtile* (200 tons). 1560

1543 (B) *New Bark* (200 tons – galleass). Listed as a ship from 1549. 1565

1544 (B) *Swallow* (200 tons – galleass). Listed as a ship from 1549. Sold 1603

1545 (C) *Mermaid* (200 tons – galleass). Captured from the French. 1563

1545 (B) *Greyhound* (200 tons – galleass) Listed as a ship from 1549. Wrecked 1562

1546 (P) *George* (80 tons – galleass). Listed as a ship from 1549. 1558

1546 (B) *Tiger* (160 tons – galleass). Listed as a ship from 1549. 1605

1546 (B) *Bull* (160 tons – galleass). Listed as a ship from 1549. 1589

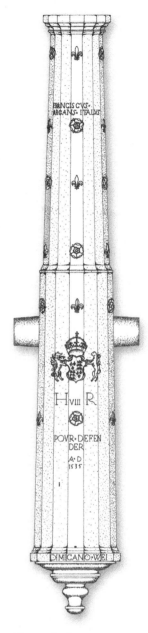

A bronze demi-cannon, recovered from the wreck of the *Mary Rose*. It was cast by the Italian gun founder Francisco Arcanus in his foundry in Blackfriars in London in 1536. The barrel was just over 8ft long. (Drawing by Rudi Roth, author's collection)

larger-calibre curtows (an early form of cannon), by the end of Henry's reign the range of guns had grown. They were still divided into the same two main groups – culverins and cannons – but both groups were further sub-divided by bore and size, producing demi-culverins and demi-cannons, as well as other smaller culverin variants – sakers and falcons. A variant of the bronze cannon was the cannon perrier, a stone-shotted weapon with a large bore and short barrel. This range of gun types would increase during the decades that followed Henry's death in 1547.

Cast-iron muzzle-loading pieces

Cast-iron pieces were being produced in England from the start of Henry VIII's reign – in 1509 cast-iron swivel guns were delivered to the *Sovereign* – but the limitations of iron founding meant that no serious attempt was made to cast larger pieces until the last years of Henry's reign. By the mid-1540s technological improvements, combined with the new war with France, led Henry to encourage domestic founders in the Weald area of south-east England to attempt the production of large cast-iron pieces. There was already a demand for cast-iron guns as a cost-effective means of arming merchant vessels, and so Wealden gun founders such as Ralph Hogge and Peter Baude rose to the challenge. The first trickle of cast-iron pieces were delivered to the Tower of London in 1545, although there is no evidence that any of these were delivered to the fleet before Henry's death. However, the iron foundries of the Weald were already producing cast-iron shot for Henry's warships, and thousands of roundshot and lagrange scraps (grapeshot) were being delivered to Henry's ordnance stores. By the 1540s the cost-effectiveness and destructive capabilities of cast-iron shot meant that stone shot – which required expensive skilled labour to produce – had been relegated to an obsolete novelty.

THE *GREAT BARK* (II), 1547

One of the most interesting major additions to Henry VIII's fleet was the *Great Galley*, which was built in Greenwich in 1515. Her design had been influenced by French and Venetian examples, and she marked a new departure for Henry's fleet – a warship that combined a full sailing rig with the ability to propel herself using oars. Her armament was originally listed as 97 guns, of which most were swivel pieces. Although she had originally been clinker-built, she was re-planked in the carvel manner during a refit in 1523, which allowed her to be pierced with gunports. Almost two decades later in 1542 she was completely rebuilt, and her oar deck given over to heavy ordnance. At the same time she was renamed the *Great Bark*. By that stage her armament included 23 heavy guns. She remained in service until 1562. The inset shows a swivel gun typically fitted to all such warships.

SPECIFICATIONS – *GREAT BARK* (II)

Type: A galleass, originally called the *Great Galley*. Built 1515 (Greenwich). Sometimes known as the *Great Galleass*, from 1542 she was known as the *Great Bark* or *Great Galleon*.

Displacement: 800 tons.*

Keel length: 100ft approx.

Beam: 25ft approx.

Armament: 87 guns (23 heavy, the rest swivel guns).

Crew (1512): 140 men (including 130 soldiers and 30 gunners).

Service notes: Rebuilt 1523 and 1542. Participated in the battle off Portsmouth. Renamed *Edward* (1547), and destroyed by accidental fire in 1553.

* In 1542 she was rebuilt as a 500-ton sailing warship.

Gun carriages

The gun carriages recovered from the *Mary Rose* constitute our one incontrovertible source of evidence on gun mounting, although other near-contemporary European shipwrecks have added to a general understanding of the way guns were mounted on board Renaissance warships. The large wrought-iron port pieces were mounted in wooden beds – more akin to hollowed tree trunks than carriages – and this form of mounting is supported by other gun carriage evidence from French and Spanish shipwrecks. All the *Mary Rose* pieces were mounted on a pair of wheels, either spoked like carriages on land, or else on smaller solid wooden truck wheels. For their part the bronze guns recovered from the wreck were all mounted on more modern four-wheeled truck carriages, all of which appear to have been designed specifically to fit that particular barrel. In general terms these carriages resembled those found on 17th- and 18th-century sailing ships of war, although the wheels were larger than those found on later carriages. Both the wrought-iron and bronze pieces would have been run forward when the ship sailed into battle, and were lashed to the hull of the ship, where the shock of the discharge would have to be absorbed by the hull timbers rather than dissipated by a controlled recoil of the gun and carriage.

Naval gunnery and tactics

The first limitation on naval gunnery was the ability of a gun to be loaded and fired. Wrought-iron breech-loading pieces were relatively straightforward, as all that was needed was to remove the powder chamber, fit a new projectile into the breech, then fit the loaded chamber back into place. An experiment involving a replica piece showed that the operation could be undertaken by a crew of four gunners, and would take five to ten minutes to complete. Swivel guns functioned in much the same way – the tankard-shaped chamber was removed, and replaced with a fresh one after the charge was loaded. This could be done by one man, and took less than a minute.

By comparison, large bronze muzzle-loading guns were cumbersome to operate, and slow to load. Evidence from the *Mary Rose* shows that there was very little space available to pull the piece back for reloading, and the cramped conditions made it virtually impossible to reload the piece in the conventional way. It was easier to leave the tip of the muzzle projecting through the small gunport, and for the loader to lean out and try to load the piece by working through the gunport. An alternative was 'outboard loading', a seemingly suicidal operation that involved the gunner clambering outside the hull of the ship, perching on the barrel of his gun, and loading it that way. There is substantial evidence that this was practised, although evolutions of this kind would invariably have taken a lot of time to complete. Similarly, the cramped conditions of the guns, and the relatively small size of early Tudor gunports compared with those of the Elizabethan period, all conspired to reduce accuracy as well as rate of fire. Therefore the evidence suggests that while it was theoretically possible to reload a ship's main guns during an action, these restrictions meant that the

A bronze 'bastard' culverin, recovered from the wreck of the *Mary Rose*, along with its four-wheeled oak carriage. The gun was cast by the English gun founders Robert and Owen in their London foundry in 1537. (Drawing by Debbie Fulford, Mary Rose Trust)

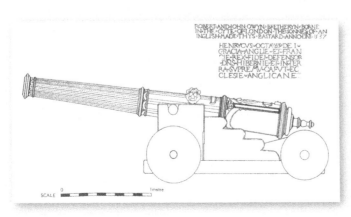

process was not readily considered a tactical option. These ships were simply not designed to engage in a long-range gunnery duel. Instead, guns were designed to fire a massed broadside immediately prior to coming alongside an enemy, and then soldiers and sailors would fight a boarding action.

In 1545 the *Mary Rose* was typical of the other major warships in the Navy Royal, carrying almost as many soldiers as it did sailors (185 soldiers to 200 mariners and 20 gunners). These troops were armed with ranged weapons (mainly longbows, augmented by a few handguns) and mêlée weapons (pikes and bills), while everyone on board, sailors or soldiers, would have some form of knife or dagger, if not a sword or axe. Some 2,000 arrows were recovered from the *Mary Rose*, the majority grouped in sheaves of 24 arrows apiece. With an archer complement of around 50 men, this gave each longbowman 30–40 arrows, which would probably have been fired in a massed 'arrow storm' during the final minutes before initiating a boarding action. Like the guns, the bows and arrows were designed to cut down enemy boarders, or to weaken the resolve of the defenders before the crew launched themselves on board the enemy vessel.

The galleass *Tiger* of 160 tons, as depicted in the *Anthony Roll*, drawn up the same year she was completed. A sister ship of the *Bull*, the *Antelope* and the *Hart*, she carried her guns on a flush main deck, the guns set above the line of oar ports for the ship's sweeps. (By permission of the Master & Fellows, Magdalene College, Cambridge).

THE TUDOR FLEET IN ACTION

Henry VIII's Navy Royal only fought two fully fledged naval engagements – one off Brest in 1512, and the other off Portsmouth in 1545. A comparison of the two battles reveals a lot about how the fleet evolved during Henry VIII's reign, and how warships were supposed to function in action.

On 10 August 1512, an English fleet of 25 ships, under the command of Sir Edward Howard, attacked a French force of similar size, commanded by René de Clèrmont. The majority of ships on both sides were armed with swivel guns or handguns rather than larger pieces of ordnance, although both the English flagship, *Mary Rose*, and the French *Marie la Cordelière* both carried 15 heavy guns apiece. Both fleets approached each other in line abreast, then individual ships broke ranks and sped on ahead to engage the enemy. In other words, all semblance of order quickly broke down, and the battle became a mêlée between individual ships, or between small groups.

A wooden crate containing longbows is excavated and cleaned, soon after its recovery from the wreck of the *Mary Rose*. So far a total of 137 yew longbows have been raised from the shipwreck. Evidence suggests they were tipped with horn. (Mary Rose Trust)

Howard's flagship, the *Mary Rose*, engaged the French flagship, *Grande Louise*, bringing down her mainmast in a close-range broadside. Consequently René de Clèrmont withdrew from the fight, and many of the other French captains followed his lead. Soon only the *Nef de Dieppe* and the powerful *Cordelière* remained, surrounded by English ships. After some seven hours the smaller French warship managed to break through the ring of five English ships that surrounded her and so managed to escape. The *Cordelière* wasn't so lucky. She managed to thwart two boarding attempts by outmanoeuvring her rivals, first by the crew of the *Sovereign* and then the *Mary James*. Then the challenge was taken up by the *Regent*,

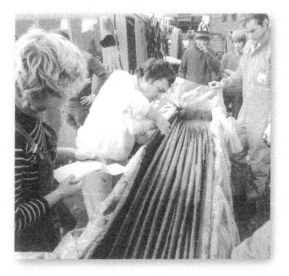

Regent and *Marie la Cordelière* at the battle off Brest, 1512. In this crude contemporary image the English warship is shown in the foreground, and flames from the French ship have already caught hold. Despite its simplicity the artist has attempted to show the substantial heavy ordnance carried by the *Regent* on her gundeck. (Stratford Archive)

the largest warship in the Tudor fleet. The boarders drove the Frenchmen from the upper deck, but then on the verge of victory came disaster. A fire broke out on the French ship and within minutes the *Cordelière* was ablaze. The rigging of the *Regent* and the *Cordelière* had also become entwined, and the English ship was unable to free herself. Inevitably the fire spread, and soon both ships were consumed by the flames. Only 20 Frenchmen survived the disaster, although 120 English sailors were rescued from the flames.

It was a dismal end to a scrappy battle, but the engagement did contain portents of the future for those willing to look for them. First, the success of the *Mary Rose* demonstrated the effectiveness of large pieces of ordnance – her guns proving to be the key to victory. It was clear that the future of naval warfare lay in the development of naval artillery, and in discovering the best way in which these guns could be used. Smaller guns also proved their worth – the *Nef de Dieppe* managed to keep the English at bay using her smaller pieces and so prevent any boarding attempt. Swivel guns were highly effective in this close-range kind of fighting, especially if enough spare chambers were on hand to keep up a heavy rate of fire. In effect they acted like machine guns, laying down a defensive barrage designed to prevent any enemy boarding party from gaining a foothold on the decks of the defending ship.

Of course there were other lessons to learn too, ones that looked backwards rather than those that focused on the new technology. For the most part the English fought in the same way as they had at the battle of Sluys (1340), relying on missile fire and hand-to-hand combat to win the battle. Throughout the Tudor period the fleet augmented its heavier firepower with soldiers, trained both to engage an enemy using longbows, crossbows or handguns to thwart enemy boarding attempts, and to take the fight to the enemy. Contemporary illustrations as well as archaeological evidence show that boarding nets were rigged to form a protective canopy over the waist of the ship – the most likely place where a boarding attempt would be made. The forecastle and sterncastle structures also bristled with swivel guns and hand-held projectile weapons, the structures acting as bulwarks in much the same way as would the ramparts of a castle. In other words, naval warfare in the early Tudor period was a strange mixture of the old and the new.

G   **THE SINKING OF THE *MARY ROSE* OFF PORTSMOUTH, 1545**

This scene is based on the well-known Cowdray House engraving (see page 45, top) showing the French attack on Portsmouth on 19 July 1545. In the original a squadron of four French galleys is shown firing on the English fleet as it closes with them to give battle. These galleys fired their guns then retired to reload – a tactic similar to the caracole manoeuvre used by contemporary pistol-armed cavalrymen. Our two deviations from the engraving involve the *Matthew Gonson* and the *Mary Rose*. In the original only the masts of the *Mary Rose* can be seen above the water, while small boats race to pick up the pitifully small number of survivors.

Our version shows the moment when the *Mary Rose* began to sink, the water filling her gundeck ports. Sir Gawain Carew on board the *Matthew Gonson* was close enough to hail his uncle on board the *Mary Rose*, when Sir George Carew reportedly called out that 'I have the sort of knaves I cannot rule'. We have therefore brought the nephew's ship a little farther forward. In the background, the *Henri Grace à Dieu* can be seen firing her bow guns at the French galleys.

Henry VIII's admirals certainly tried to learn their lesson. While the king concentrated on improving the heavy armament of his ships, his admirals tried to work out how to use these new guns to their best advantage. To help them the Tudor lawyer Thomas Audley produced a set of tactical guidelines in 1530, roughly midway between the two main battles fought during Henry's reign. Although he was no seaman, Audley tried his best to wrestle with the problem of gunnery, and his *Instructions* show the perceived wisdom of the time, albeit based largely on the experiences of the fight off Brest.

He advocated that gunfire be reserved for close range, and that boarding actions only be attempted after the upper decks and fighting tops of an enemy vessel had been cleared of defenders using artillery, swivel guns and archery. Although he also recommended gaining the 'weather gauge', in other words taking an advantageous position upwind of the enemy, Audley understood that any battle would soon degenerate into a mêlée in which individual ships attempted to board those of the enemy. The only suggestion of any higher coordination came in his recommendation that pinnaces be used to ferry reinforcements from one ship to another. This was hardly innovative – merely the reflection of existing practices.

An altogether more useful set of guidelines was published by the Spaniard Alonso de Chaves in the same year, but probably only reached England 13 years later, when the Spanish ambassador presented a copy of *Espejo de Navegantes* (The Mariner's Mirror) to Henry VIII. Translations were soon

English ships sailing out of Portsmouth harbour to do battle with the French. This detail of the lost Cowdray House painting shows some of the smaller vessels of the fleet, those displacing less than 200 tons. Interestingly, each vessel is shown towing its ship's boat astern of her. The original painting was destroyed by fire in 1793. (Stratford Archive)

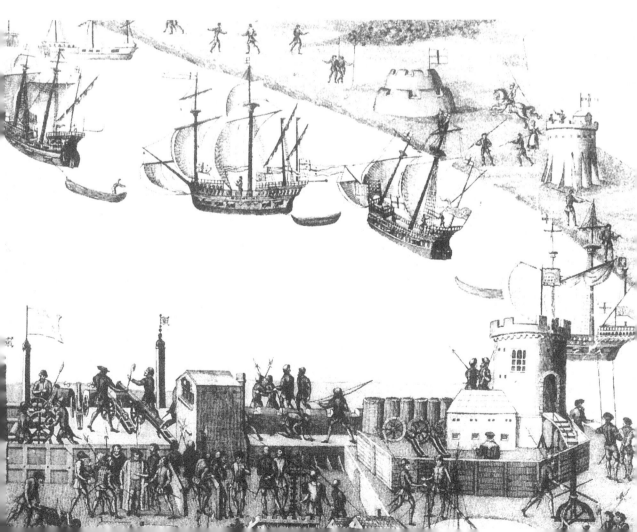

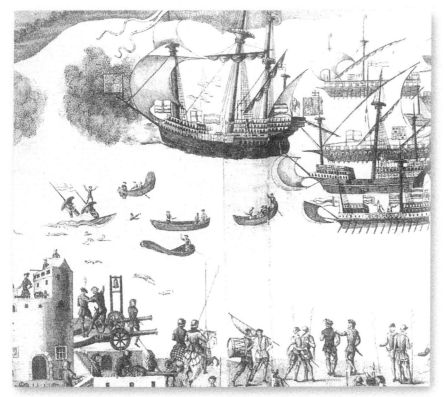

Another detail of the Cowdray House painting of the Battle off Portsmouth in 1545, this captures the scene moments after the *Mary Rose* sank – her masts can still be seen in the foreground – while the *Henri Grâce à Dieu* is still engaging the French galleys using the guns on her port bow quarter. The sailing ships and galleasses of the rest of the fleet can be seen coming to the rescue of the *Mary Rose*'s survivors. (Stratford Archive)

passed on to Henry's fleet commanders. De Chaves advocated dividing the fleet into two groups. The larger ships were designed to board the enemy in the old way. They would be supported, however, by a squadron of smaller warships operating on the flanks of the main force, which would harass the enemy using long-range artillery fire. Here was the breakthrough – the origin of the school of English naval tactics that would come into its own during the reign of Queen Elizabeth I. By the 1540s it had already become possible to fire a broadside at long range, and then to reload it before closing with an enemy. What the de Chaves guidelines advocated was the deliberate use of long-range fire as a tactic in its own right.

Two Tudor warships in a sea battle – a detail reproduced from the *Carta Marina* of Olaf Magnus, 1539. Just as in the engagement between the *Mary Rose* and the *Louise* in 1512, a shot has brought down the mainmast of one of the vessels. This prompted the French flagship to retire from the fight. (Stratford Archive)

The opportunity to try out this new doctrine came in the summer of 1545, when Tudor England faced the threat of a French invasion. A French fleet of 225 ships commanded by Admiral Claude d'Annebault entered The Solent – the waterway separating the Isle of Wight from the English mainland. Roughly a quarter of this armada were transport ships, carrying a French army of 30,000 men. On 19 July Admiral Viscount Lisle led Henry's Navy Royal of around 100 ships out of Portsmouth harbour to give battle. That morning the French admiral had sent forward a squadron of galleys, which lay off Gosport and bombarded the English fleet at long

List of ordnance, from William Harrison's *An Historical Description of the Iland of Britaine*, which introduced *Holinshed's Chronicles* (1587)

Gun type	Calibre (in.)	Gun weight (lb)	Shot weight (lb)	Powder charge (lb)	Point-blank range (paces)
Old cannon	7	8,000	42	60	400
Cannon	8	7,000	60	20	400
Demi-cannon	6½	6,000	30	28	760
Culverin	5½	4,000	18	18	500
Demi-culverin	4½	3,000	9	9	400
Saker	3½	1,500	5	5	360
Minion	3¼	1,100	4½	4½	340
Falcon	2½	800	2½	2½	320

range. The English foray may well have been Viscount Lyle's response to this goading. Then – without any warning – French observers saw the *Mary Rose* heel over and sink. No doubt the French gunners imagined they were responsible. In fact, the venerable Tudor warship was heavily laden, and her gunports were close to the waterline. A sudden strong gust heeled the ship over, the water poured into the open ports, and the ship foundered within minutes. The English Vice Admiral Sir George Carew and 700 of his men went down with their ship.

When the French galleys retired from their skirmish, the English fleet then withdrew to its anchorage. Within a week the French had gone – the English had too many forces assembled near Portsmouth to risk a landing on the mainland, so after raiding the Isle of Wight d'Annebault headed back to France, where his fleet supported the siege of the English-held port of Boulogne. The battle would have added little to our understanding of Tudor naval warfare were it not for the loss of the *Mary Rose*. Her remains provide us with a snapshot of a Tudor warship in the closing years of Henry VIII's reign, and provide evidence of just how far the Tudor navy had come during the past three decades. While she still carried a complement of archers and soldiers, and her anti-boarding net had been rigged, the *Mary Rose* possessed a powerful broadside armament.

Even though the design of the ship probably precluded her participation in an extensive naval gunnery engagement due to the cramped conditions on board, she would have been a formidable opponent, capable of capturing an enemy through a devastating broadside fired at point-blank range, followed by a spirited assault on an enemy vessel once its defenders had been whittled down by gunfire and archery. As such she represents a transitional period in naval warfare. She was designed to fight a boarding action, yet she possessed the guns needed to pound away at an enemy using firepower alone. However, it was not until after the death of Henry VIII that the Tudor Navy Royal would begin to favour naval gunnery over hand-to-hand combat. It would be the seamen who served Henry's daughter Elizabeth who would fully embrace the new technology, and it would be under Elizabeth that the Tudor fleet finally emerged as the most powerful naval force of its age.

FURTHER READING

This list is not supposed to be an extensive bibliography, but more a small selection of books that will allow the subject to be explored in greater depth. All are readily available in good bookshops and libraries. For a detailed list of less widely available sources, see Konstam (2008), below.

Caruana, Adrian B., *The History of English Sea Ordnance, 1523–1875: Vol. 1 – The Age of Evolution, 1523–1715*, Rotherfield, Jean Boudriot (1994)

Gardiner, Robert (ed.), *Cogs, Carvels & Galleons: The Sailing Ship, 1000–1650*, London, Conway Maritime Press (1994)

Glete, Jan, *Warfare at Sea, 1500–1650: Maritime Conflicts and the Transformation of Europe*, London, Routledge (2000)

Guilmartin, John F. Jr, *Galleons and Galleys*, London, Cassell (2002)

Howard, Frank, Dr, *Sailing Ships of War, 1400–1860*, London, Conway Maritime Press (1979)

Jones, Mark (ed.), *For Future Generations: Conservation of a Tudor Maritime Collection*, Portsmouth, Mary Rose Trust (2003)

Knighton, C. S., & D. M. Loades, *The Anthony Roll: Henry VIII's Navy*, London, Ashgate (2000)

Konstam, Angus, *Sovereigns of the Seas: the Quest to Build the Perfect Renaissance Battleship*, Hoboken, Wileys, NJ (2008)

Landström, Björn, *The Ship: An Illustrated History*, London Doubleday (1961), reprinted as *Sailing Ships in Words and Pictures*, Doubleday (1978)

Loades, David, *The Tudor Navy: An administrative, political and military history*, Aldershot, Scolar Press (1992)

Marsden, Peter, *Sealed by Time: The Loss and Recovery of the Mary Rose*, Portsmouth, Mary Rose Trust (2003)

Nelson, Arthur, *The Tudor Navy: the Ships, Men and Organisation, 1485–1603* London, Conway Maritime Press (2003)

Oppenheim, Michael, *The History of the Administration of the Royal Navy from 1509 to 1660*, London (1896), reprinted by Temple Smith (1988)

Rule, Margaret, *The Mary Rose: the Excavation and Raising of Henry VIII's Flagship*, London, Conway Maritime Press (1982)

The galleass *Greyhound* of 200 tons was just one of eight mid-sized galleasses built by Henry VIII in anticipation of a war against France. The king saw them as a means of countering the powerful French galley fleet. This depiction of her in the *Anthony Roll* was produced the year she entered service with the fleet – a year after the battle off Portsmouth. (By permission of the Master & Fellows, Magdalene College, Cambridge)

In addition, the author's Master's thesis *Naval Artillery to 1550: An analysis of its design, development and employment* (University of St. Andrews 1985) may be acquired through academic library loan, while an abstract of the section on Tudor naval gunnery was published in *Guns at Sea*, London, Royal Armouries Conference Proceedings (1988).

INDEX

References to illustrations are shown in **bold**.